February

K. C. KELLEY • BOB OSTROM

The Child's World

Published by The Child's World®
1980 Lookout Drive • Mankato, MN 56003-1705
800-599-READ • www.childsworld.com

Acknowledgments
The Child's World®: Mary Berendes, Publishing Director
The Design Lab: Design
Jody Jensen Shaffer: Editing and Fact-Checking

Photo credits
© bikeriderlondon/Shutterstock.com: 10; Boykung/Shutterstock.com: 6; EdStock/iStock.com: 19 (top); Georgios Kollidas/Dreamstime.com: 18; Jerry Coli/Dreamstime.com: 23 (bottom); JoseIgnacioSoto/iStock.com: 20 (top); Jpainting/Dreamstime.com: 19 (bottom); Luis Carlos Jimenez del rio/Shutterstock.com: 13 (top); Michael Pettigrew/Shutterstock.com: 12 (top); NASAPhoto by Bill Taub: 20 (bottom); PictureLake/iStock.com: 22 (bottom); s_oleg/Shutterstock.com: 13 (bottom); Suzanne Tucker/Shutterstock.com: 11 (top); tratong/Shutterstock.com: 11 (bottom); Vezzani Photography/Shutterstock.com: 12 (bottom); Wikimedia Commons: 22 (top)

ISBN 9781626873650
LCCN 2014930704

Printed in the United States of America
Mankato, MN
July, 2014
PA02214

ABOUT THE AUTHOR

K.C. Kelley has written dozens of books for young readers on everything from sports to nature to history. He was born in January, loves April because that's when baseball begins, and loves to take vacations in August!

ABOUT THE ILLUSTRATOR

Bob Ostrom has been illustrating books for twenty years. A graduate of the New England School of Art & Design at Suffolk University, Bob has worked for such companies as Disney, Nickelodeon, and Cartoon Network. He lives in North Carolina with his wife and three children.

Contents

WELCOME TO FEBRUARY!

Poor February! All the other months have at least 30 days. The second month of the year has just 28 (or 29) days. It's always the shortest month of the year. But that just makes it special! February brings groundhogs and valentines. Maybe February's not so bad after all!

FEBRUARY

FACT BOX

Order: Second

Days: 28 (or 29)

WHY ALL THE LEAPING?

Every four years, February has 29 days, not 28. That happens in Leap Years. Why the extra day? Each day on Earth is actually a little bit longer than 24 hours. And each year is slightly longer than 365 days. So the extra time doesn't build up, every four years, we add another day to the year. That balances out the calendar and puts us back on track with time. We "leap" ahead in time with the extra day!

HOW DID FEBRUARY GET ITS NAME?

The ancient Roman calendar had only 10 months. In about 150 BCE, Emperor Pompilius changed it to 12. He added two months: January and February. At the beginning of the second new month, Romans cleaned up. They got themselves ready for a religious feast. Romans spoke Latin, and the Latin word for cleaning up, or purifying, is *februare*.

Birthstone

Each month has a stone linked to it. People who have birthdays in that month call it their birthstone. For February, it's amethyst.

FEBRUARY AROUND THE WORLD

Here is the name of this month in other languages.

Chinese	Èr yuè
Dutch	Februari
English	February
French	Février
German	der Februar
Italian	Febbraio
Japanese	Nigatsu
Spanish	Febrero
Swahili	Februari

THE REAL STORY OF A SHORT MONTH

The Roman emperor Pompilius made February 29 days long at first. One month had to be shorter, and he picked that one. But it didn't last long. Another emperor came along later and took one of February's days away. The eighth month of the year was named in honor of Caesar Augustus, but it was just 30 days long. Being a big-time emperor, he wanted his month to be as long as the others. He took a day away from February, making February 28 days and August 31 days.

BIG FEBRUARY HOLIDAYS

Groundhog Day, February 2

An old legend says that a groundhog in Punxsutawney, Pennsylvania can tell the weather. If the groundhog sees its shadow in the morning, there will be six more weeks of winter. If it doesn't, spring will be here soon.

HAPPY BIRTHDAY, PRESIDENTS!

Two of America's greatest presidents were born in February. George Washington was born February 22, 1732. Abraham Lincoln was born February 12, 1809. In 1971, the U.S. government declared the second Monday in February to be a

Valentine's Day, February 14

February 14 is the celebration of Saint Valentine. He was a priest who lived more than 1700 years ago. Saint Valentine performed marriages when it was against the law. For more than 700 years, people have been greeting those they love on this day. Today, more than one billion Valentine's Day cards are sent each year. The holiday is celebrated in the United States, Canada, Mexico, and even England.

SUPER BOWL!

The biggest sporting event of the year now usually comes in February. The Super Bowl is the championship game of the National Football League. The first Super Bowl was in January of 1967. Starting in 2004, the Super Bowl moved to a Sunday in early February.

FUN FEBRUARY DAYS

February has more ways to celebrate than just sending cards on Valentine's Day! Here are some of the unusual holidays you can enjoy in February:

EARLY FEBRUARY

National Girls & Women in Sports Day

FEBRUARY 9

National Stop Bullying Day

FEBRUARY 11

National Inventors' Day

FEBRUARY 15

National Hippo Day

FEBRUARY 20

Love Your Pet Day

FEBRUARY 22

World Thinking Day

FEBRUARY 24

National Cupcake Day

World
Pistachio Day

FEBRUARY 28

National Tooth
Fairy Day

FEBRUARY WEEKS AND MONTHS

Holidays don't just mean days…you can celebrate for a week, too! You can also have fun all month long. Find out more about these ways to enjoy February!

FEBRUARY WEEKS

Boy Scout Anniversary Week: The Boy Scouts of America were founded on February 8, 1910. Scout troops around the country have celebrations this week. More than 100 million boys have been Scouts over the years.

Children's Authors and Illustrators Week: During the first week of February, writers and artists who work for children say thanks. They visit schools and libraries. Teachers talk to kids about books and reading. Some classes even write thank-you notes to authors.

FEBRUARY MONTHS

African-American History Month: African-Americans have made many contributions to the United States. This month, we celebrate that. The holiday started in 1915. A group of teachers started "Negro History Week." The word Negro was an old word used to describe people of African **heritage**. It's not used today.

Over time, students and teachers began to use the week to look at black Americans' works and deeds. The important events of the **Civil Rights Movement** were talked about. The sad history of slavery is always part of the lesson.

In 1976, President Gerald Ford declared February to be "Black History Month." The name has changed to its current name. What is your class doing to celebrate?

FEBRUARY AROUND THE WORLD

Countries around the world celebrate in February. Find these countries on the map. Then read about how people there have fun in February!

FEBRUARY 3

Bean Throwing Day, Japan

It's called *Setsubun* in Japanese. On this day, people welcome the coming spring by throwing beans. They say, "In with fortune! Out with demons!" Legend says that throwing the beans chases away demons.

THE FOURTH OF FEBRUARY?

America's Independence Day is July 4. Some countries celebrate their freedom in February. Sri Lanka, Grenada, Lithuania, Gambia, St. Lucia, Estonia, and the Dominican Republic all have Independence Days in February.

Tet, Vietnam

Some Asian countries have a second calendar. It counts the years differently than in the West. In Vietnam, the first day of their new year is called *Tet*. It's the biggest holiday of the year. People go to parades and parties. They also visit graves of their relatives to honor them. Tet sometimes occurs in January.

Waitangi Day, New Zealand

On this day in 1840, New Zealand settlers and the native Maori people signed a peace agreement. Today, New Zealand points to this day as the start of its nation. Some Maori, however, look back on this as a sad day in which natives gave up their land.

FEBRUARY IN HISTORY

February 1, 1790

The U.S. Supreme Court met for the first time.

February 4, 1789

George Washington was elected as the first President of the United States.

"DO YOU BELIEVE IN MIRACLES?"

That's what reporter Al Michaels said after a hockey game on February 22, 1980. The game was one of the biggest sports upsets ever. At the Winter Olympics, the U.S. hockey team beat the mighty Soviet Union, 4–3. America's heroes later won the gold medal. No one thought the U.S. could win. For U.S. fans, the win was a miracle!

Queen Elizabeth II of Great Britain was crowned in London.

The first U.S. postage stamps were introduced.

February 16, 1923

King Tut's tomb in Egypt was opened for the first time in 3,000 years.

February 20, 1962

John Glenn became the first person to **orbit** the Earth. The American astronaut whizzed around the globe three times.

NEW STATES!

Three states first joined the United States in February. Do you live in any of these? If you do, then make sure and say, "Happy Birthday!" to your state.

Oregon
February 14, 1859

Massachusetts
February 6, 1788

Arizona
February 14, 1912

FAMOUS FEBRUARY BIRTHDAYS

February 4

Rosa Parks

In Mississippi, she refused to give up her seat on a bus. She became a symbol and a leader in the Civil Rights Movement.

February 6

Babe Ruth

"The Bambino" was the greatest slugger in baseball history. He played 21 seasons for the Boston Red Sox and New York Yankees in the 1920s and 1930s.

February 11

Thomas Edison

Are you reading this under a light? Thank Edison, inventor of the light bulb.

February 15

Susan B. Anthony

She fought to give women the right to vote. For her work, she was the first woman put on an American coin—it is worth $1.

February 17

Michael Jordan

Most experts think he is the best basketball player of all time. "Air Jordan" won six MVP awards and 10 NBA scoring titles.

GLOSSARY

Civil Rights Movement (SIV-il RYTS MOVE-ment) Civil rights are a person's rights to freedom and equal treatment. The Civil Rights Movement focused on winning equal treatment for blacks from the mid-1950s to the late 1960s.

heritage (HAYUR-ih-taj) Heritage is someone's cultural background and traditions.

legend (LEJ-end) A legend is a story that has been handed down from earlier times.

orbit (OR-bit) To orbit something means to travel all the way around it.

INDEX